alchemy

Kaylee Oh

BookLeaf
Publishing

Presentation by *BookLeaf Publishing*

Web: www.bookleafpub.com

E-mail: info@bookleafpub.com

ISBN: 9789395756570

First edition 2022

DEDICATION

To the recovering perfectionists, the former catastrophizers, and everyone in between.

cold

/kōld/ adj

1. the blue we painted our bedroom wall the night your grandmother died
2. aching, delicate joints; flares
3. toe-deep pools that collect after floods
4. refreshingly, summer rains
5. you have her now
6. the words "but" and "because"
7. lavender-scented candles
8a. cortisone shots in the spaces between bones
  b. genetic predispositions; positive Rheumatoid factors
9. archaic: raspberry-stained lips on the carotid; pulses racingLove Story I

Escapement

Last night, we ran out.
Alarms rang
from behind spring-
loaded faces,

so we opened
up the moon, dipped
our fingers into cogs
and gears and black
grease. We smeared
time on walls
and thighs, left

dirty cereal bowls
in the kitchen sink.
Last night, we were miners,

digging for quartz
in craters. We opened
a bottle of red wine
with a screwdriver. We sifted
pieces of cork
through our teeth. We counted

seconds by swings

of ceiling fans
above couches and unmade
beds and sun-stained
patio furniture.

Outside, a couple
stood under streetlamps
so far away they could have kissed
and we never would have known.
Time watched,
hands folded. We stitched

the moon
together with red thread
and greasy fingertips
and hung it in the neighbor's
backyard.

Woman

She was designed with
brush strokes and
pot smoke, tendrils
that turned into curves,
formed her practically
transparent.
I loved the moment
before she said my
name, how she would let it float
on her lips.
I wanted to touch her
with the tips of my fingers,
wanted to let
my name stain
my hands with the pink
lipstick she loved to leave
on the collars of my shirts.
Her tongue was a
foreign language and I wanted
to learn every word
I could. I wanted to
draw maps across
her body,
wanted to catch
each perfect ringlet of smoke

as she exhaled and
keep her sweet breath
in the pocket of
my jeans.

Love Story I

From Words to Live By (2008)

"You can make a man love you by
putting a lock of your hair in his shoe"

      he's been pulling
      hair out of his socks
      for days now and he still wakes
      up next to her

Show Me the Way Home, Honey

We locked the doors and windows while
we watched the sun sink below
the top level of the parking garage, airplane
lights
blinking through fogged-with-breath
windshield. They streaked
across the sky, leaving neat
lines, running parallel
and perpendicular:
      coordinate
      mapping history,
      silent touches
      and embarrassed blushes across
the hood of Dad's old
car. We didn't touch.
Instead, we held on to jet
engines booming against
tinted glass,
watched giant metal birds
cradle thousands of hearts
in their wings,
taking them to different places
to see so many
things.

Moonshine

Someone stole rings
off planets last night
and never put them back.
Saturn grieved their cost,
while Jupiter cursed his luck
and searched unmade bed
sheets. The sun

came up west
and set east.
No one noticed,
but truck drivers
and the doctor smoking
outside after her shift
while you sipped tequila
and fruit punch from a blue cup,
alone, because all at once,
everyone was gone. Your God says

he made planets
and can take what he pleases,
        everyone keeps saying so
but your frostbitten fingers
say it was you.

Wanted: Ad 236

Week of March 17

Woman who finds faith
in the ocean seeks
man who wants to wake up
with sand between his toes.

Mangrove

They stretch, long
spindly legs
dragging through water,
pressing into earth.

They reach high,
strong arms
lifting green through broad breezes
into sky.

In the quiet
afternoon sun,
they are alive,
sipping brackish
water through
rooted straws.

Wanted: Ad 255

Week of March 24

Man with flames
for cheeks
seeks woman who wants
to wake up with smoke
in her hair.

Love Story II

From Words to Live By (2008)

"You can make a man love you by putting
his picture on a table and burning a candle on
top
of it for nine days"

     the wax dripped until
     I couldn't see
     his face
     the candle was too small
     it stopped
     burning
     after four and a half

warm

/wôrm/ adj

1. white yarn I continue to buy and then spill things on
2. being serenaded on an AstroTurf lawn
3. nine am at twelve thousand feet
4. your sleeping bag before the chipmunks chewed holes in it
5. sore calves
6. questions asked and answered through only a glance
7a. our clothes fresh from the dryer
  b. the smell of laundry detergent
8. Christmas trees just off the truck (snow still tucked into the branches)
9. the campfire I have penned into my skin (a reminder of that night; see: burned)

Wanted: Ad 687

Week of August 11

Couple seeks books
of matches,
jet-setting seashells,
wedding planner.

this is a love poem, but not for you

i.
the fire

burned my photographs–
a shoebox worth,

but you saved the
negatives.

they're pressed to the window
in my kitchen.

stained glass
on a cathedral wall.

ii.
you still come up in conversations
about love. honey-smooth
and warm,
sometimes it
presses against my stomach, that word,

love,

like frozen peas
against bruised knuckles,
cold and hard,
but soothing.

iii.
you twisted the ends

of my hair
at the dinner table

and, later,
you kissed me,
the hot sleepy skin
of my spine.

I never thought much

about faith
until then.
and I would have turned over,
but my mouth tasted like beer
and you thought I was asleep.

iv.
i want to know you

because you
are not a part of me

we are not
two halves
of a whole.

we are two separate entities,
wearing shoes
coated in cooking oil,

never able to stay
on our feet.

hot

/hät/ adj

1. ends of hair too close to candlelight
2. kimchi on rice; fingers too stiff for chopsticks
3. red pepper flakes; jalapeño; bitten tongues;
wasabi
4. waves rising off pavement
5a. informal: desire; ache and skin on skin on
skin
  b. i wish knew how to touch in such an
innocent way
6. microphones, left on, picking up backstage
conversation
7. tropical breezes; ocean water
8. radiation; radiating; radioactive
9. trouble bubbling like lava: parking tickets,
      car accidents, unrequited love

Love Story III

"Always try to resolve
issues with your partner
in bed"

   she built a barrier
   between us
   with pillows
   but once she's asleep
   I trace "I love you"
   into the bare
   skin between her shoulder blades

On Goodwill Wedding Dresses

i.
beaded bodice
braced against thin-
lipped kisses.

ii.
bright flower girl eyes
watch as bouquet
slips through
bridesmaid hands.

iii.
poems scrawled on the backs
of pay stubs
and old coffee shop receipts.
my eyes have never
been so dwelled upon.
i will never marry
another writer.

iv.
i wonder if he came
in here and saw

my dress marked
to only twenty dollars,
muddied hem
and lost sequins
glowing,
city lights over an angry ocean,
if he would finally
leave.

Love Story IV

"There is a point where crying
over a lost
lover is more about your ego
than your heart"

      he wasn't lost
      so much as gone
      and she still has scars
      on her knees
      from the broken window
      from the bedroom rug
      from the Sunday
      morning hangover
      too strong to have come from booze

old fashioned

here, love, press your heart to mine let them beat
together against one another each other can
yours slow mine can mine speed yours catch
your breath, love, we can sit for hours listening
to the sound of inhale and exhale pause and let it
rinse you clean we can go back to normal some
other time for now this is the shake breathe with
me press yourself against me lace your fingers
with mine i can keep time with your pulse under
my palm delicate skin counting each beating
moment catching and twisting and aching for
touch and taste and mouth and hand and pacing
through the darkened house pressing against
walls silent silent silent when will it start again
we will never be sure we may never know where
or when or what but we know who who who

And there they were,

pressing lips to hand, arm,
shoulder, raspberry-burnt cheeks while
    the sun   stretched across
    the water,   rendering
    the sand   almost blue.